XTREME FISHING

BIG GAME
FISHING

BY S.L. HAMILTON

A&D Xtreme
An imprint of Abdo Publishing | www.abdopublishing.co

Visit us at
www.abdopublishing.com

Published by Abdo Publishing Company, a division of ABDO, PO Box 398166, Minneapolis, Minnesota 55439. Copyright ©2015 by Abdo Consulting Group, Inc. International copyrights reserved in all countries. No part of this book may be reproduced in any form without written permission from the publisher. A&D Xtreme™ is a trademark and logo of Abdo Publishing Company.

Printed in the United States of America, North Mankato, Minnesota.
102014
012015

 PRINTED ON RECYCLED PAPER

Editor: John Hamilton
Graphic Design: John Hamilton
Cover Design: Sue Hamilton
Cover Photo: Corbis
Interior Photos: Alamy-pgs 8-9, 9, 11 & 26; AP Images-pgs 13, 18-19 & 23; Corbis-pgs 12, 14, 16-17, 22-23, 26-27 & 29; iStock-pgs 1, 2-3, 4-5, 6, 7, 10, 14-15, 18, 20, 20-21, 24-25, 28-29, 30-31 & 32.

Websites
To learn more about Fishing, visit booklinks.abdopublishing.com. These links are routinely monitored and updated to provide the most current information available.

Library of Congress Control Number: 2014944874

Cataloging-in-Publication Data

Hamilton, S.L.
  Big game fishing / S.L. Hamilton.
    p. cm. -- (Xtreme fishing)
  ISBN 978-1-62403-679-8 (lib. bdg.)
  Includes index.
  1. Big game fishing--Juvenile literature.   I. Title.
  799.16--dc23

2014944874

Contents

Big Game Fishing

The deep waters of Earth's oceans and seas hold monster-sized fish. Big game anglers seek the thrills and excitement of hooking powerful fighters such as barracuda, tuna, and sharks.

Barracuda

Big game fish are known for their strength and speed. They can reach sizes of more than 1,500 pounds (680 kg).

XTREME FACT – Big game fishing is also called blue-water fishing or deep-sea fishing.

Boats and Gear

Big game fishing requires big boats and special heavyweight tackle and gear. Many anglers charter boats with experienced captains and crew members. Local captains know their home waters and the best spots to find fish. Big game fishing often requires long trips to deep waters, often 100 miles (161 km) or more.

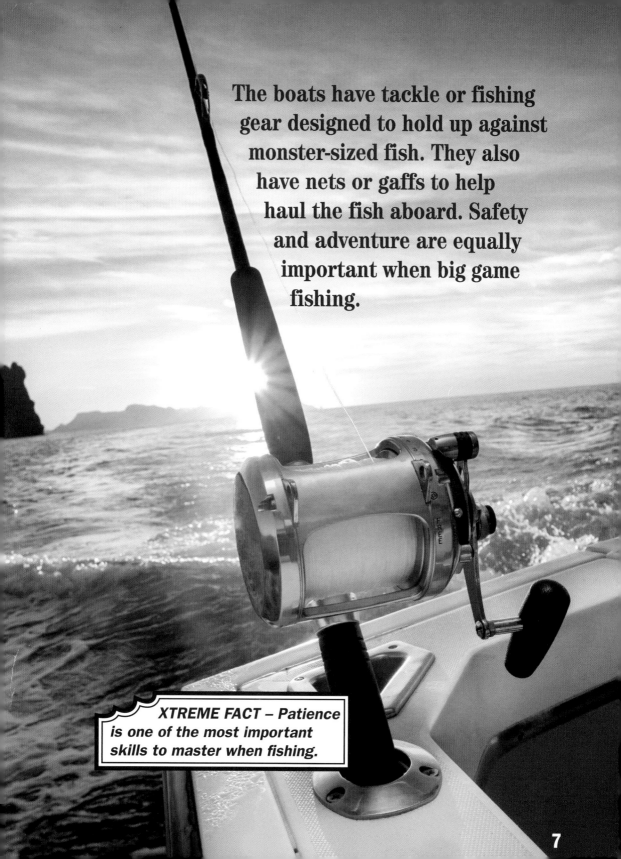

The boats have tackle or fishing gear designed to hold up against monster-sized fish. They also have nets or gaffs to help haul the fish aboard. Safety and adventure are equally important when big game fishing.

XTREME FACT – Patience is one of the most important skills to master when fishing.

Marlin

Marlin are the most sought-after big game fish. They are named after their coloring: blue, black, white, and striped. When hooked, marlin are violent fighters, often jumping, twisting, and swimming away at speeds greater than 50 mph (80 kph). Many anglers say that catching a marlin is the prize of their lives.

XTREME FACT – A billfish is any fish that has a long, spear-like bill or snout. These include marlin, sailfish, and swordfish.

To catch these fish, anglers slow-troll using live bait and heavy tackle, or high-speed trolling lures. Marlin often weigh more than 1,000 pounds (454 kg). Special gear is required just to haul these monster fish into the boat.

Blue Marlin

Sailfish

Atlantic sailfish weigh about 140 pounds (64 kg), while Pacific sailfish grow almost double that size, about 220 pounds (100 kg). Most anglers troll for these great fish using live bait. The bait swims excitedly as a sailfish closes in. Sailfish strike with great force. When hooked, the fight is on between angler and fish! Sailfish jump, tail walk, and cartwheel across the water's surface until they are finally reeled in. Since sailfish are rarely eaten, many are released back into the ocean.

XTREME FACT– Sailfish mounted for display do not use any parts of the actual fish. Photos and dimensions are taken, and then the fish is released. Fiberglass reproductions are made by a taxidermist. This is known as a "release mount."

Swordfish

Swordfish have a long, flat bill resembling a sword. They are difficult to find, but swim in the tropical waters of the Atlantic, Pacific, and Indian Oceans. They usually weigh between 200 to 1,000 pounds (91 to 454 kg). Females are larger than males.

XTREME FACT– Bait must be sewn on with rigging twine to the hook, or the swordfish will knock it loose.

Anglers get swordfish strikes by trolling with bait such as whole bonito, mackerel, or large squid. Hooks are dropped deep below the surface. Once hooked, these hard-hitting fish will run and surface, performing a series of jumps and acrobatic moves that anglers never forget.

A 683-pound (310-kg) swordfish caught off the Florida Keys in 2012.

Bluefin Tuna

Bluefin tuna are one of the largest fish in the sea. They are also one of the most delicious. Unfortunately, this has resulted in severe overfishing. Strict fishing limits on this slow-growing species are in place today. Many sport fishermen release their catch, hoping to help the bluefin tuna population rebound.

Adult bluefin tuna can weigh from 500 to 1,000 pounds (227 to 454 kg). They are found in the Atlantic and Pacific Oceans, as well as the Gulf of Mexico. The largest fish are drawn to chummed waters near an anchored boat, where fishermen hook them with jigs. Others troll the water with spreader bars baited with mackerel or squid.

XTREME FACT – *In 2014, a Japanese restaurant owner paid $70,000 for a 507-pound (230-kg) bluefin tuna. The fish are used in Japanese sushi and sashimi dishes.*

Yellowfin Tuna

Yellowfin tuna may not grow as large as their bluefin cousins, but they still reach sizes of 300 to 400 pounds (136 to 181 kg). Because they are fast growers, anglers are free to hunt them in the offshore waters surrounding the United States.

Trolling with lures such as spoons or cedar, plastic, and chromed jigs often results in strikes. Other fishermen chum the water to attract yellowfin. Once a school is spotted, anglers bait their hooks with squid, butterfish, or anchovies. When a big yellowfin strikes, it puts up an exciting fight.

Great White Sharks

Sharks will eat almost anything. They have razor-sharp teeth and powerful muscles. Of all the sharks in the sea, the most prized by fishermen is the great white shark. To catch these fierce predators, anglers chum the water with oily fish such as herring or mackerel, which attracts scent-sensitive sharks. Hooks are baited with chunks of decaying fish. The smellier the bait, the more likely a shark will come to investigate. Some fishermen tie the bait to a hook using rigging line or dental floss. This prevents sharks from simply taking it off the hook.

XTREME QUOTE – "Treat all sharks with great care, even hours after they are caught, and absolutely never place any body parts, hands and feet especially, near their mouths."
—Milt Rosko, saltwater fisherman and author

Mako Sharks

Makos are the race cars of sharks. They swim at speeds up to 50 miles per hour (80 kph). Their sleek, streamlined bodies perform abrupt twists and turns. When hooked, they can jump 20 feet (6 m) into the air, somersaulting and spinning as they try to escape. For big game anglers, a mako shark on the line is an awesome challenge.

XTREME FACT– Although many sharks do not taste good, makos are considered to be delicious.

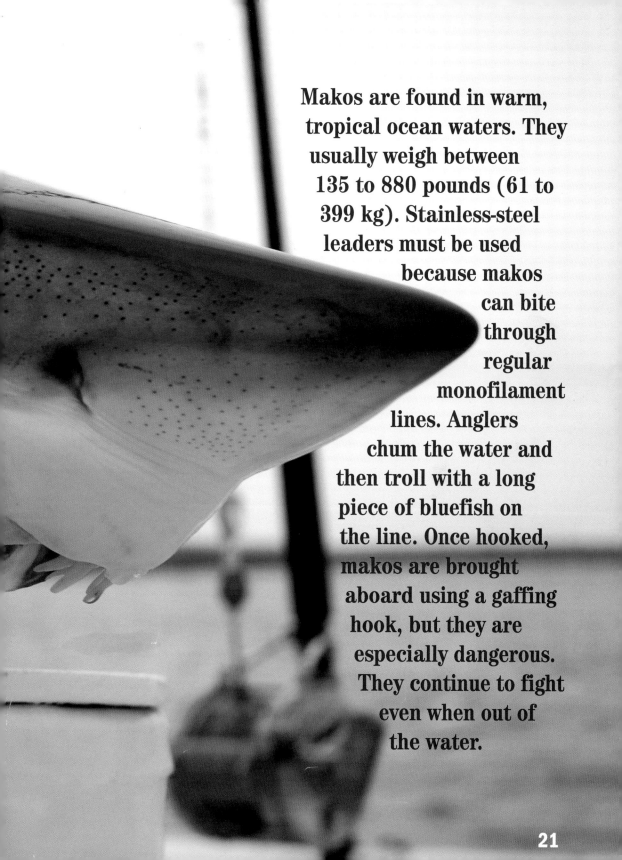

Makos are found in warm, tropical ocean waters. They usually weigh between 135 to 880 pounds (61 to 399 kg). Stainless-steel leaders must be used because makos can bite through regular monofilament lines. Anglers chum the water and then troll with a long piece of bluefish on the line. Once hooked, makos are brought aboard using a gaffing hook, but they are especially dangerous. They continue to fight even when out of the water.

Thresher Sharks

Thresher sharks are easily recognized by their long whip-like tail, or "caudal fin." A thresher uses its caudal fin to herd its prey into a group. It then slaps the fish to stun them before swallowing them. Because threshers use their tails in this manner, they are often snagged in the tail when slapping a baited hook. Threshers are found in ocean and coastal waters worldwide. Some thresher species are protected, but many are fished. They weigh between 300 and 1,000 pounds (136-454 kg).

Anglers troll for thresher sharks with hooks baited with mackerel, or they use lures. When hooked, threshers will fight, often surprising anglers with great bursts of speed. They are one of the few fish that can breach, leaping completely out of the water.

XTREME FACT – Most experienced anglers advise against removing a hook from a live shark's mouth. If practicing catch-and-release, it is important to use a circle hook instead of a j-hook.

Dorado

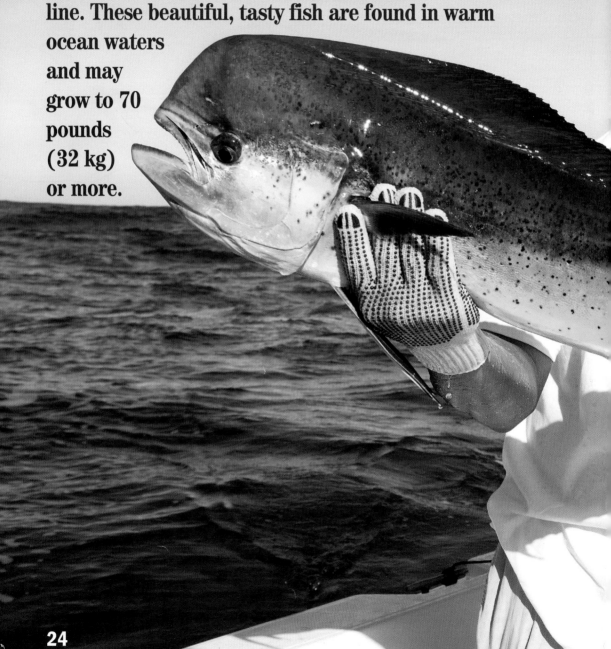

When brilliant tones of yellow, blue, and green are spotted, anglers know that a dorado is on the line. These beautiful, tasty fish are found in warm ocean waters and may grow to 70 pounds (32 kg) or more.

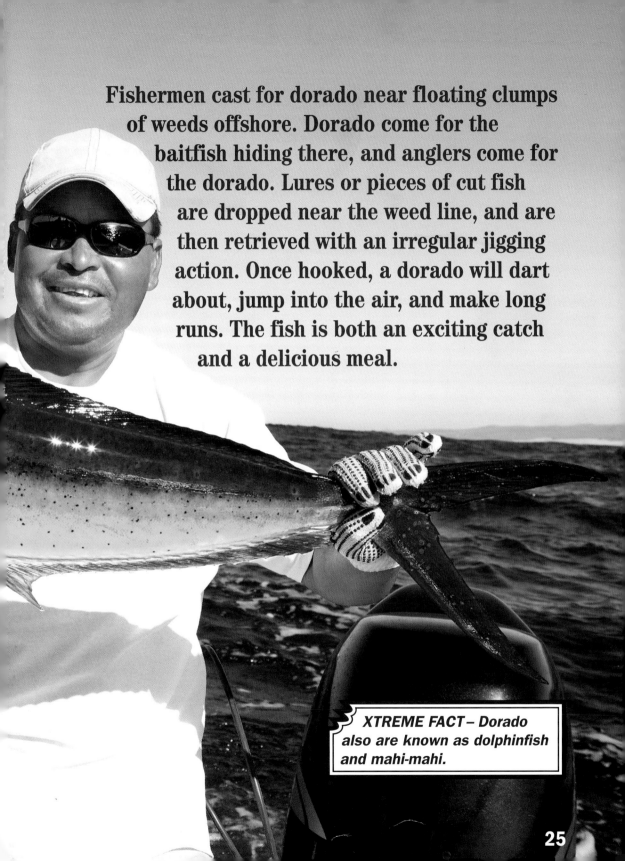

Fishermen cast for dorado near floating clumps of weeds offshore. Dorado come for the baitfish hiding there, and anglers come for the dorado. Lures or pieces of cut fish are dropped near the weed line, and are then retrieved with an irregular jigging action. Once hooked, a dorado will dart about, jump into the air, and make long runs. The fish is both an exciting catch and a delicious meal.

XTREME FACT – Dorado also are known as dolphinfish and mahi-mahi.

Tarpon

Tarpon are air breathers. When hooked, they are not afraid to take their fight from the blue waters into the blue sky. Many anglers consider tarpon to be the greatest aerial jumping fish.

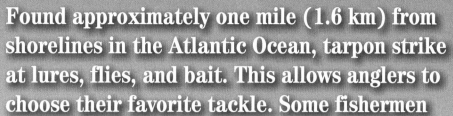

Found approximately one mile (1.6 km) from shorelines in the Atlantic Ocean, tarpon strike at lures, flies, and bait. This allows anglers to choose their favorite tackle. Some fishermen will anchor their boats at an area where tarpon are known to gather. Others prefer to search for the silver fish in open waters. Once hooked, a tarpon will jump and fight. Although not monster-sized, these fish usually weigh between 50 and 150 pounds (23-68 kg). Record-sized tarpons can weigh nearly 300 pounds (136 kg).

XTREME FACT – Tarpons are also called "silver kings" because of their coloring.

Dangers

Deep-water fishing can be dangerous. The weather can change quickly. Rough seas or a damaged boat or motor are possibilities. Seasickness, dehydration, and sunstroke are also hazards.

Big fish can pose big dangers. People have been speared by billfish and bitten by sharks. Having respect and using caution for the fish and the open seas are important for any big game angler.

Glossary

Billfish

A large sport fish with a long, pointed bill, or snout. Marlin, sailfish, and spearfish are billfish.

Breach

When fish jump out of the water.

Chum

Bait consisting of blood and fish parts that is thrown into the water to attract game fish.

Gaff

A long, sturdy pole with a hook on one end, used to spear large fish and lift them out of the water and into boats. Gaffs are used when fish are so large they might break fishing poles or line.

Jig

A type of fishing lure. Jigs are lead sinkers with hooks built in, and covered with a colorful body to attract fish. Fishermen move jigs in a jerky, up-and-down motion to coax fish into biting the lure.

Sport Fish

A fish that anglers hunt because of its fierceness and difficulty in landing, making its capture an exciting sport.

Spreader Bar

Several artificial lures attached to a short wire and dragged, or trolled, through the water. The group of lures resembles a school of small fish. The last lure in the group has a hook in it. Sport fish are attracted by the group of lures and react by attacking the trailing lure, possibly because it resembles the weakest or most vulnerable fish in the school.

Streamlined

The shape of a creature or object that reduces the drag, or resistance, of air or water flowing across its surface. This increases speed and ease of movement. Certain fish, such as sharks and marlin, have a streamlined shape that allows them to swim faster because they don't have to push as hard to move through the water.

Tackle

Equipment used by fishermen, such as rods, reels, hooks, lines, and sinkers. Tackle is often kept in a tackle box.

Tail Walk

When a fish appears to "walk" across the surface of the water on its tail.

Troll

To fish by trailing a baited hook and line behind a moving boat.

Index